P9-BBN-686

To: Carol and all our Family and Friends

From: Jaff & Chuslaves

Dec. - 25 - 2006

To my beloved grandchildren, Angelia,
William, and Jeffrey, who are the loves of my life.
— *Sylvia Browne*

To my wonderful children, Angelia and
William, who make every day like Christmas for me.
— *Chris Dufresne*

Special thanks to Linda Rossi

Text copyright © 2006 Sylvia Browne and Chris Dufresne
Scripture taken from the New King James Version.
© 1991 by Thomas Nelson, Inc. used by permission.
All rights reserved
First U.S edition 2006
Printed in China

Browne, Sylvia.
Christmas in Heaven / by Sylvia Browne and Chris Dufresne.
Edited by Kat Shehata; design by Jo McElwee

p.cm.

ISBN 0-9777790-0-9
1. Christmas. 2. Heaven. 3. Spiritual life.
I. Dufresne, Chris. II. Title.

BV45.B74 2006 263'.915
QBI06-600113

Angel Bea Publishing
www.angelbea.com

Christmas in Heaven

by Sylvia Browne and Chris Dufresne

Gift-giving is a wonderful Christmas tradition

In fact, even spirits and angels give gifts to Jesus on Christmas Day. Let's all take time this year to make Christmas a religious celebration, not just a retail holiday. As Christians, may we all remember the true meaning of Christmas and honor our Hosts of Heaven by loving one another.

— *Sylvia Browne and Chris Dufresne*

Christmas is a joyous celebration commemorating the birth of Jesus Christ. This Christian holiday is rich in traditions such as decorating pine trees with ornaments and lights, exchanging gifts among friends and family members, and singing classic songs created for the season. Christmas is not *just* a festive occasion for people on earth. Christmas is also celebrated in Heaven on December 25th in the presence of Mother God and Father God, the Son, and the Holy Spirit.

— *Sylvia Browne*

In your mind, create the most exquisite environment you can imagine

The weather is perfectly warm with gentle breezes.

The people you loved throughout your life

are with you, smiling and laughing.

No one is in pain, angry, or confused.

You feel important and loved.

— *Chris Dufresne*

This is Heaven

Heaven looks just like earth in its most natural, unspoiled beauty

There are mountains, oceans, rainforests, and natural wonders like the Grand Canyon. Even our most precious man-made treasures exist in Heaven.

— Sylvia Browne

Every living thing that God created exists in Heaven

All the wonderful species of plants,

trees, and animals that we know

and love from our lives on earth

as well as an infinite number

of living things that we

can only dream of exist

in perfect harmony

on the Other Side.

— Chris Dufresne

People of all races and colors are one family

There is no prejudice or tension. There is only love. Every person is wonderfully different and unique in his or her own way. God loves everyone equally. Our spirits spend eternity enjoying the company of the world and the people we love. We go to parties, visit art galleries, and attend book readings. There are also movie theaters, tennis courts, and football stadiums.

— *Chris Dufresne*

There are billions of spirits and angels in Heaven

The difference between spirits and angels is that spirits are the souls of people like you and me, while angels are a separate phylum of beings created by God to serve as warriors in His army. There are ten different levels of angels all created to serve a specific purpose for God. For example, there are Archangels, like Michael, who serve as messengers, Powers who have the ability to heal, and Cherubim and Seraphim angels who spread joy by singing and playing music.

— *Sylvia Browne*

Christmas
in
Heaven

Imagine the most beautiful sunset you have ever seen, a garden full of roses in perfect bloom, and Roman columns accented with green vines. Picture yourself together with the people and animals you have loved throughout your lifetime mingling with angels in paradise. Now see yourself standing in the presence of God. The scene you just created is not a fictional place. This is an area in Heaven called The Rose Garden.

This is where Christmas is celebrated on the Other Side

— *Sylvia Browne*

Rose Garden at Christmastime

All God's creations—people, angels, animals, and even nature—have a role in preparing for Christmas. The Rose Garden is always breathtakingly beautiful, but even more so at Christmastime.

— *Chris Dufresne*

Butterflies with iridescent wings

enter the garden bringing with
them new vibrant color each time
they flap their wings. Fireflies nestle
in trees, emitting a golden glow
to the colorful backdrop.

— *Sylvia Browne*

(Butterflies and fireflies are the only
insects I have seen on the Other Side.)

People share the same gift-giving traditions in Heaven as we do on our side

As you might imagine, gifts given to Jesus are treasures beyond our wildest dreams. Like a hand-made gift a child gives to her parents, the gifts people give to Jesus on His birthday are special to Him because they are the epitome of gifts from the heart.

— *Chris Dufresne*

On Christmas morning in The Rose Garden, all the spirits of Heaven gather together

Cherubim and Seraphim angels fill the sky playing instruments and singing heavenly songs. The music is familiar to all so everyone joins the angels in song while they anticipate the main event: the re-enactment of the nativity scene.

— Sylvia Browne

In place of a manger, the nativity scene is re-enacted in a beautiful golden palace

Mary sits in the palace holding her newborn baby boy with Joseph by her side. Animals gather around the newborn King just as they did in Bethlehem. Mother and Father God are present in all their glory for all to see.

— *Sylvia Browne*

Mary stands with an infinite league of angels around her. She raises her arms to God and presents to Him a golden ball of light. The golden ball of light intensifies and from the light Jesus appears as a grown man before all of Heaven. It is as if He has been incarnated from a baby to the man He grew to be in life.

— *Sylvia Browne*

Jesus is God's gift to the world

Everyone rejoices as the miracle of Jesus' birth unfolds before their eyes

The air is filled with white doves

and every kind of bird you could imagine.

They fly in formations creating circles and

making crosses, all giving homage to our Lord.

— *Chris Dufresne*

Spirits and angels rejoice

as Jesus ascends to His throne with His Father on the left and His Mother standing to His right. People form a line before Jesus, eager to give Him their special gift.

— *Sylvia Browne*

What gift is worthy of Jesus?

Some people offer the Lord hand-made gifts, paintings, songs, poems, or other artistic works.

Others present Jesus
with colored balls of light,
like the golden ball of light Jesus
ascended from in Mary's arms.

Each colored ball of light can be described as a manifestation of faith. Each represents a good deed performed during our lives, an act of faith, or a testimonial. This heavenly ritual is similar to our Christian tradition of standing up in church and "testifying" our faith and love for the Lord before the congregation. When someone gives Jesus a light, they are essentially affirming to Jesus, testifying if you will, that during their lifetime, they carried His spirit, had faith, and carried out His mission of helping others.

— *Sylvia Browne*

What will you give to Jesus?

WHITE CHRISTMAS

The weather on the Other Side is perfect in every way. The temperature is eternally warm with gentle breezes and there are no storms or threatening weather conditions. While the temperature is always around 78 degrees, there is snow in Heaven. Snow in Heaven is not cold and icy like it is on our side. It is actually warm and fluffy!

— *Sylvia Browne*

Gifts
from
the
heart

LTY

COMMITMENT

The greatest gift we can give to Jesus in our lifetime
is to "love one another" (John 15:12).
We don't have to wait until we go Home to show Jesus
our gratitude, loyalty, and commitment to Him.
— *Sylvia Browne*

GRATITUDE

To be grateful for not only our life, but
also the fact that God gave us the
opportunity to learn in this world
so we can ascend to a higher level.

— *Sylvia Browne*

Loyalty

To be zealous and
accountable, not
only to God, but
to each other.
To keep our
focus on what is
righteous and
good and
never waver.
— *Sylvia Browne*

COMMITMENT

To be committed
to our path

whether full of

joy or sadness,

and to never

waver in

our goal

to do good.

— Sylvia Browne

Jesus dedicated His life to helping others

It stands to reason then

that the best possible

gift you could give

Him in return is to

emulate His

spirit of giving.

— *Chris Dufresne*

Move

Mountains

In the spirit of giving

Volunteer at your church, become a mentor to a child, donate to worthy charities, be a positive role model to others, spend time with your loved ones so they feel your love and commitment.

— Chris Dufresne

Start a new tradition in your family this year that centers around Christ. On Christmas Eve, bring your family together and light a candle. Talk about the highlights of the past year. What are you grateful for? What hardships did you overcome? What would you like to achieve by next Christmas? Pray together as a family. Thank Heaven for all your blessings.

— Chris Dufresne

PRAY

"For where two or three are gathered together in my name, there am I in the midst of them."

(Matthew 18:20)

Talk to your children about the first Christmas

Help them understand what the

celebration is all about.

Christmas is becoming so

overcommercialized that our

future generations may not

remember the true

meaning of Christmas.

— *Chris Dufresne*

Forgiveness

"For if ye forgive men their trespasses, your heavenly Father also will forgive you; but if ye forgive not men their trespasses, neither will your Father forgive your trespasses."
(Matthew 6: 14-15)

"And all things, whatsoever ye shall ask in prayer, believing, ye shall receive."

(Matthew 21:22)

The Golden Rule

Do unto others
as you would
have them
do unto you.

*"And as ye would that men should do to you,
do ye also to them likewise."*
(Luke 6:31)

Christmas

Traditions

ALBUM

Think about the most memorable Christmas gifts you ever received

Did you receive an answered prayer on Christmas Day, like having your whole family together? Or a sentimental gift from a family member or friend, such as a knitted scarf, a photograph from your childhood, or a family heirloom passed down to you? Chances are, the most precious and endearing gifts we receive throughout our lives are not bought in stores.

— *Sylvia Browne*

Family
Traditions

What sights, smells, and sounds of the season
bring back fond memories of Christmas? Write
down these traditions in a journal and add
pictures or cards that you kept over the years.
Keep adding new pictures and mementos
every year to keep your family traditions
alive for future generations.

— *Chris Dufresne*

Give a thoughtful gift: An orange

Precious family Christmas traditions have been lost or diminished over the years. My Grandma Ada, born in Germany in 1865, had a wonderful tradition in her family. On Christmas morning, everyone received an orange. Then, her family and friends got together and spent the day singing Christmas carols, playing games, and eating Christmas dinner. The orange was a wonderful gift, as they were hard to come by at this time. But the true excitement on Christmas Day was not centered around gifts, but rather the fellowship and worship among family and friends.

— *Sylvia Browne*

While Christmas is usually an exciting and joyous occasion, all of us have, or will at some time, experience the loss of a loved one. This is extremely painful and it seems even more difficult around special occasions like birthdays, anniversaries, and Christmas. It may seem to you that the person who died is "gone". Our loved ones are always with us. Not only are the ones we love symbolically in our hearts and in our memories, but their spirits come to us in dreams and to our side when we need to feel the warmth of their eternal love. Ask your loved ones to come to you so that you can feel the eternal warmth of their spirit. Share Christmas memories about them with your friends and family. Make a special ornament in their memory and hang it on your tree. Remember, life is everlasting.   — *Chris Dufresne*

You will be reunited with your loved ones on the Other Side

Christ is always with us

Throughout our lives Christ is available to all who speak His name. Although most of us will never actually see Him as a physical form in our lifetime, we can feel His presence. In Heaven, at any given time, you can see Jesus at church, sitting on a bench having a one-on-one conversation with someone, or just enjoying the company of His eternal family.

— *Sylvia Browne*

Go Home
for Christmas

Have you ever gone to bed with a problem and woke up with a logical solution to work it out? Have you ever had a dream about a deceased loved one that felt so real you would swear it really happened? This is because our spirits visit Heaven as we sleep. While we are on the Other Side, we work out our problems, visit with our family members, and give ourselves a break from the negativity that surrounds us in our world. When you go to sleep on Christmas Eve, say a prayer, and spend Christmas in Heaven. Ask God that you will remember something from your visit.

— *Chris Dufresne*

Christmas is not the only holiday celebrated on the Other Side. High holy days of other religions are also commemorated with great celebration. Whether it's Buddhism, Islam, Judaism, etc., everyone has their day of celebration. In Heaven, religion doesn't exist like it does here. Religion, simply put, is the spiritual love of God. People carry with them "cell memories" (knowledge and experiences from our lifetimes). For this reason, spirits find it comforting to celebrate their feast days of Passover or other ceremonies they have experienced in life. In Heaven, we carry with us our memories of earth, but there are no conflicts with each other or theological arguments. In fact, many people participate in all different religious ceremonies.

— *Sylvia Browne*

Regardless of how you choose
to celebrate this Christmas,
remember what the occasion
is all about: the birth of
Jesus Christ, our Lord.
Remember what He taught
us through His own example:
how to love, forgive, sacrifice,
and help others. Ask yourself
this question:
What gift can I give to Jesus?

— *Chris Dufresne*

Merry Christmas

Sylvia Browne

Chris Dufresne

About the Authors

Sylvia Browne

Millions of people have witnessed Sylvia Browne's incredible psychic powers on TV shows such as *Montel*, *Larry King Live*, *Entertainment Tonight*, and *Unsolved Mysteries*. Sylvia is the author of numerous books and audios, and has recently launched her own merchandise line, The Sylvia Browne Collection. She is also the president of the Sylvia Browne Corporation and the founder of her church, the Society of Novus Spiritus.

Chris Dufresne

Chris is the son of Sylvia Browne. Like his mother, Chris is a gifted and highly respected psychic in his own right who has been in practice for more than 20 years. He is the author of *Animals on the Other Side*, *My Life with Sylvia Browne,* and *My Psychic Journey*. Sylvia and Chris both work in Campbell, California.

For more information about Sylvia Browne and Chris Dufresne, please visit their website www.sylvia.org.

Also from Sylvia Browne and Chris Dufresne

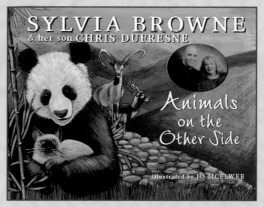

"Will my pets be with me on the Other Side?"
"I have been asked this question hundreds of times. Let me assure you we will all spend eternity with our pets and animals of every kind. As an animal lover myself (I have eight dogs!), I was inspired to write this book completely devoted to animals, called *Animals on the Other Side*."

— *Sylvia Browne*

STRENGTH
Bless my home
with the presence
of animal spirits and
totems. Let the strength,
courage, and loyalty
of animals reflect
on me and allow my
spirit to reflect their
soul's perfection.
—Sylvia C. Browne

Visit our website to see the
Sylvia Browne Collection and
sign up to receive our monthly
e-coupons and special new
product announcements.

www.angelbea.com

SYLVIA BROWNE
Light a Candle

COLLECTOR'S EDITION